This book aligned with the Next Generation Science Standards (NGSS). The Next Generation Science Standards (NGSS) are reproduced with permission from the Department of Education.

The Earth Changes Fast and Slow: Living With Waves

Student Edition ISBN 978-1-952346-49-1

By Lauren Franzen, Aysha Imtiaz, Jake Hunter, Beth Hunter and Grant Cowell.

STEMTaught® **Grade 2**
Next Generation Science

2-ESS1-1 Earth's Place in the Universe: Use information from several sources to provide evidence that earth events can occur quickly or slowly.

Featured author:

L auren Franzen
Earth Scientist
Brigham Young University

I love studying what makes the beautiful landscapes that we can see. I study geology because I like going on hikes and seeing cool rocks. Geology is fun! I study volcanoes, earthquakes and dinosaurs! Geology involves a lot of really fun field trips in the outdoors. I have been able to walk through caves that once were full of hot lava, find gemstones in a riverbed, and break open rocks to find fossils!

1

Lesson Anchor

Explore Google Earth

Practice using Google Earth to explore Earth's beautiful features.

What you'll need:

- a computer or other device

What you'll do:

Use Google Earth to view Uluru Rock, Australia.

1. Open your Internet browser and go to:

https://earth.google.com

2. Search "Uluru Rock, Australia."

3. Move the view to the side. Click and drag your mouse.

(Click, drag)

4. Tilt the view up or down. Press the "ctrl" key, then click and drag up or down ("command" key for Mac).

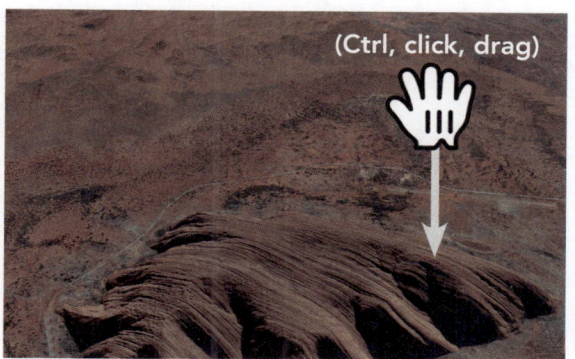

(Ctrl, click, drag)

5. Rotate the view in a circle. Press the "ctrl" key, then click and drag to the side ("command" key for Mac).

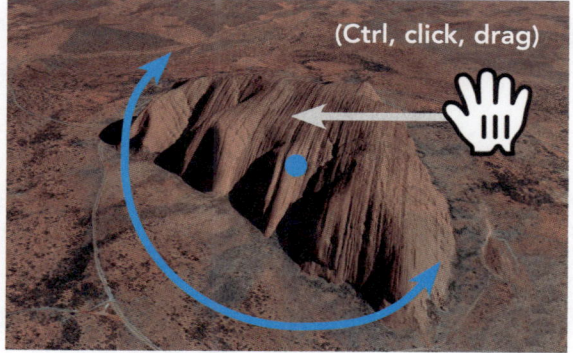

(Ctrl, click, drag)

6. Zoom in or out. Click the "+" or "-" icon, then click on the map.

click

(Click)

This is Uluru Rock, Australia

After you explore Uluru rock, draw it here.

How long do you think it takes for a mountain such as Uluru Rock to form?

 Think, Pair, Share!

Do you think Uluru Rock formed fast or slow? Why do you think so?

Does it happen fast or slow?

Glue these cards in place when you identify an Earth process that is fast or slow.

First one home wins, okay?

Okay, it's a deal! 1-2-3 go!

Some things move quickly...

... and some things move slowly.

5

The fastest things don't always win!

Each of the pictures below show a change that naturally occurred to a landscape.

Do you think these changes happen fast or slow?

Think, Pair, Share!

Don't use your "Fast" and "Slow" cutouts yet! Just discuss with your partner why you think each change happens fast or slow.

Flowing ice carves steep valleys into a mountain.

Rivers reshape the land as they carry silt, sand and rocks downstream.

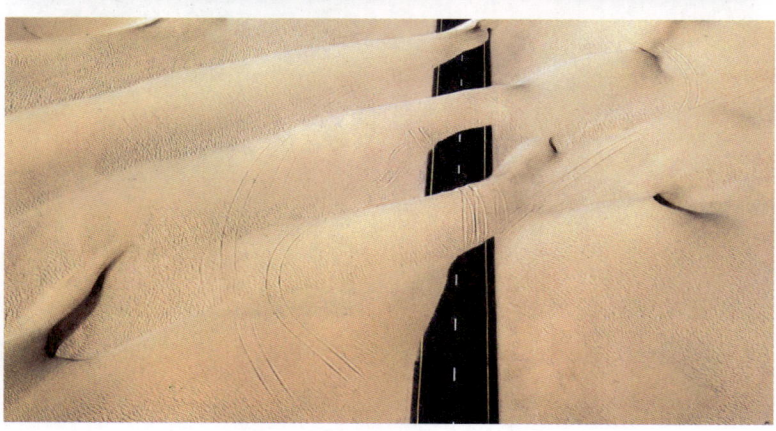

Wind blows dry sands across a desert road, forming sand dunes.

Earth's features can change

Flowing water, ice or wind can carry small pieces of earth such as silt, sand, and rock from one place to another. Erosion happens when ice, water, or wind changes the shape of the land.

Havasu Creek is slowly carving out this beautiful canyon.

Silt particles make a fine mud or clay.

Sand particles are tiny pieces of rock.

Pebbles and gravel are larger pieces of rock.

How can erosion change the shape of land?

Cut and fold the flaps to see how erosion can change the shape of land.

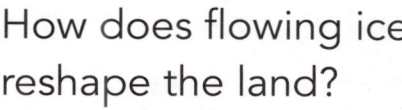

How does flowing ice reshape the land?

 Is this change fast or slow?

How does flowing water reshape the land?

 Is this change fast or slow?

How does wind reshape the land?

 Is this change fast or slow?

Fold Line

Fold Line

Fold Line

Ice carries rocks with it as it slowly flows down a mountain. When the ice melts it leaves behind steep cliffs. This process takes thousands of years.

Flowing water carries small pieces of silt, sand and rock with it as it flows downhill. The water creates slopes and valleys after thousands of years.

Wind can carry small pieces of sand as it blows. The wind creates dunes, or mountains of sand, that can quickly move across the desert. Dunes move from year to year.

Where do sediments go?

Broken pieces of rock such as sand, silt and gravel are called sediments. These materials were broken into smaller pieces by erosion. Sediments are brought down from higher ground by flowing water or ice and settle in low places to form new layers of ground.

On the photo, trace the fan shape that the new sediments formed.

Where the river leaves the steep mountains, sediments form new layers of ground in the shape of a fan.

Can you identify newly deposited sediments in this photo?

Winds quickly reshape desert sands

Wind can change a sandy desert landscape. Wind blows sand up one side of a dune and down the other. Winds can move the sand dunes of the Namib Desert up to 40 feet (12 meters) per year.

Explore:

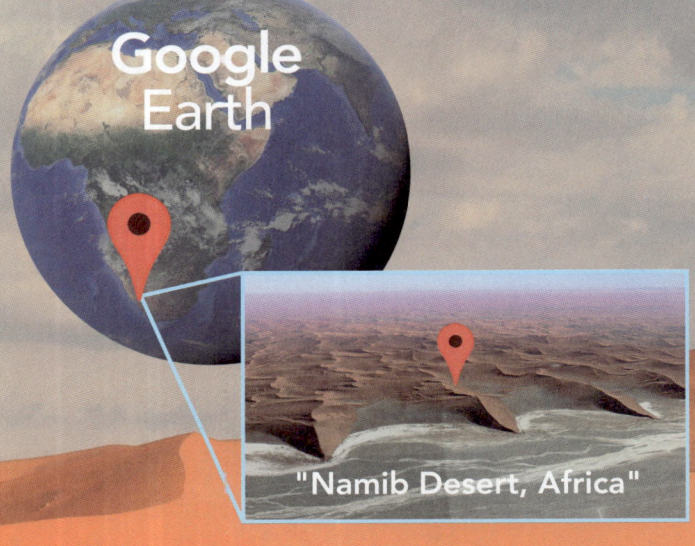

"Namib Desert, Africa"

Make a ✔ when you find it.

☐ Tall and small dunes

☐ The edge of the dunes

☐ Wavelike patterns in the sand

Dunes are made up of sand that is blown easily by the wind. Wind sorts the sediments by size. Dust is carried away and rocks are left behind. Sand is collected into huge dunes.

Are sand dunes reshaped by wind quickly or slowly?

Why do you think sand dunes are made up of sand rather than dust or rock?

Think, Pair, Share!

What size of sediments can you blow?

How does blowing wind work to change the shape of land formations such as sand dunes? Experiment to find out!

What you'll need:

- Mezzie measuring tape

- a straw

- a petri dish or plate

- Scoopy spoon

- Skilly the scale (kitchen scale)

- some sediment samples or small objects to blow (flour, salt, gravel, or sand).

What you'll do:

Step 1: Use Scoopy spoon to put a sediment sample in your petri dish.

Step 2: Observe, measure, and describe your sample.

Step 3: Blow on your sample with a straw to see how far you can move the particles.

Sand dunes are reshaped and moved by winds a little every day.

A Silt-sized Sediment

What could you use for your experiment that is like a silty sediment with dust-sized grains? Try using flour!

Flour

Flour has tiny, dust-sized grains. For your experiment, flour can be used instead of silt.

??? What's in your petri dish?

Draw your sample here.

Can you move the particles by blowing?

Yes   **No**

How far can you blow your sediment?

I love to measure!

Describe your particles. You can describe their size and weight or you could use words such as smooth or gritty.

_____

_____

_____

_____

A Sand-sized Sediment

What could you try blowing that is like a sandy sediment?
Try using sand or salt!

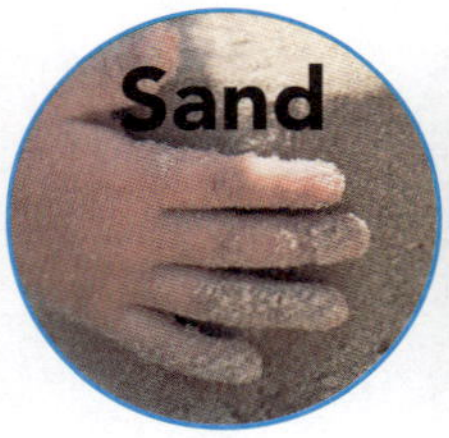

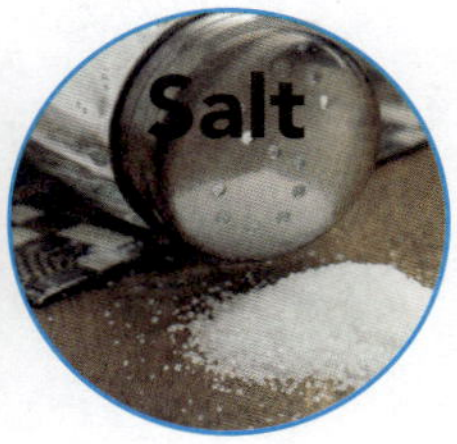

Sand **Salt**

Sand and salt have
small grains.

??? What's in your petri dish?

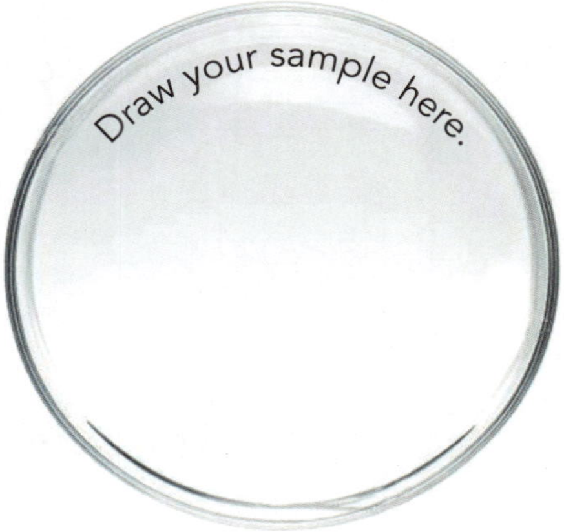

Draw your sample here.

Can you move the particles by blowing?

(**Yes**)   (**No**)

How far can you blow your sediment?

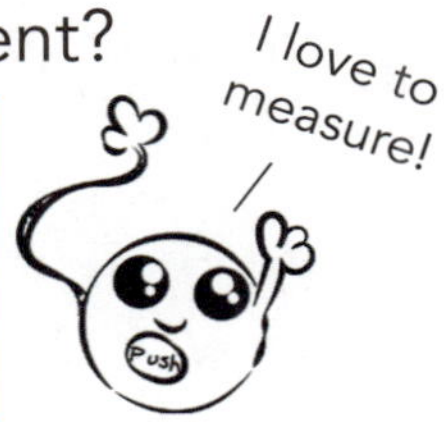

I love to measure!

Describe your particles. You can describe the size and weight or you could use words such as smooth or gritty.

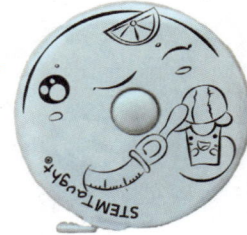

A Gravel or Rock-sized Sediment

Try moving gravel, pebbles or small rocks by blowing on them with your straw! These sediments have larger grains than silt and sand.

If you don't have gravel, pebbles or rocks, use a small object such as an eraser or wooden block.

 What's in your petri dish?

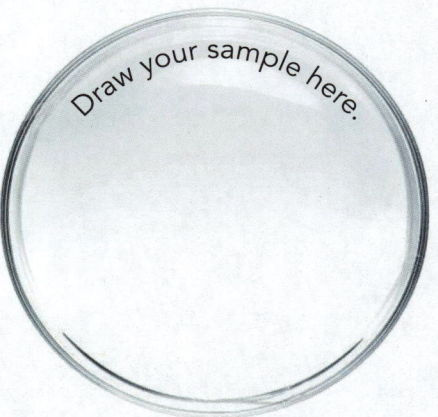

Draw your sample here.

Can you move the particles by blowing?

 Yes  No

How far can you blow your sediment?

I love to measure!

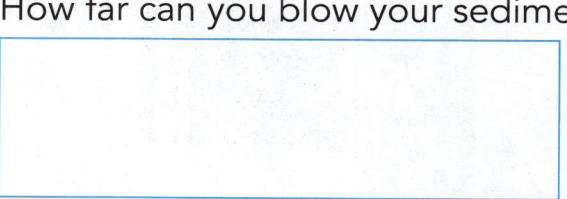 Describe your particles. You can describe the size and weight or you could use words such as smooth or gritty.

_____

_____

How do you think the size of the sediment affects the formation of dunes?

Think, Pair, Share!

Floods can reshape land quickly

A flood happens quickly when large amounts of water flow into an area. During a rainy season, rainwater can flood rivers, canyons, lakes and even cities. Floodwaters move rocks, sand and mud very quickly. Floods make the landscape look different than before.

The water flowing over Iguazu Falls, in Brazil, is normally clean and clear.

Do floods happen quickly or slowly?

Think, Pair, Share!

Does a flood happen quickly or slowly? How do you know?

During a flood, the river water is often brown with dirt and mud. Floodwaters can cut deep into riverbanks causing erosion to occur quickly.

Explore:

Google Earth

"Iguazu Falls, Brazil"

Make a ✓ when you find it.

☐ Where the river is wide

☐ Where the river is narrow

☐ A deeply cut river valley

19

Erosion slowly shaped the Grand Canyon

Water can take a long time to change a landscape. When water passes over the same spot year after year, it can break down rock and wash away sediments. After a very long time a river can create a large canyon.

Was the Grand Canyon formed quickly or slowly?

The Colorado River cut this deep river gorge over hundreds of thousands of years.

The Grand Canyon is very large and impressive. It became that way after thousands of years of erosion from the Colorado River.

Think, Pair, Share!

Was the Grand Canyon formed quickly or slowly? How do you know?

Explore:

Google Earth

"The Grand Canyon"

Make a ✓ when you find it.

☐ Colorado River path

☐ Flat, high ground

☐ Valleys with white, red and brown layers of dirt

MY NANA JANI'S BEARD

As you read the story, notice how Muntaha helps her grandfather slow soil erosion in their farm field.

Part 1

Muntaha's farm

Muntaha lives on a farm with her grandparents. She helps tend to the crops and loves to help take care of the baby goats. Before planting, Grandfather covers piles of seeds with a warm cozy blanket so the seeds won't blow away. Muntaha loves poking her fingers in the soil to plant the seeds. Muntaha wakes up early in the morning to help her grandfather. She calls him Nana Jani (grandfather dearest). They have lived happily and in the past have always had a large enough harvest to share food with their loved ones and neighbors.

Why did grandfather cover the seed piles with a blanket?

Think, Pair, Share!

Part 2
What's wrong, Nana Jani?

As the years passed and Muntaha grew older, she noticed that the baskets at harvest time were getting lighter and lighter. The harvest wasn't a happy celebration anymore. She also noticed that her grandparents seemed worried. They often gave her food to eat but claimed that they weren't hungry. Sometimes, she would see them sitting outside staring at the fields. They looked sad and worried. Her Nana Jani had stopped taking care of himself—he used to get his beard trimmed every weekend at the local barber 'shop' under a tree. But, now, he has a fuzzy beard. It tickles Muntaha when he hugs her.

Why didn't things at the farm seem to be going so well? Why do you think Nana Jani was so worried?

Think, Pair, Share!

Muntaha wanted to know what was wrong with her Nana Jani.

She asked him, "Why don't you get your beard trimmed anymore?"

Nana Jani's eyes crinkled up in a special smile which he always saved just for her. "The better to tickle you with!" he said. He swooped her up in his arms and swung her round and round.

Between giggles and squeals, Muntaha tried to ask him, "No! Nana Jani! Tell me!"

"Well," grandfather said. "My beard protects my face from the cold wind and the rain of winter just like a baby goat's thick coat of hair."

How does Nana Jani's beard protect his face?

Think, Pair, Share!

Muntaha had more questions than just that.

"Why is our harvest so small this year? Why do you sigh when you look out over our fields? Why are the wheat stalks so short this growing season?"

"Well," Nana Jani answered. "It looks like you noticed that I have some more work to do."

Before Muntaha could ask any more questions, Nana Jani rushed to the barn and started to tend to the animals.

Part 3

Empty grain sacks

Muntaha was not going to be fooled so easily. She followed him to the barn and rummaged around. She found the burlap sacks they had used a few years ago to pack wheat and grain.

In the past, the sacks were so full of grain that they were stretched tight at the seams. This year the sacks looked sad and deflated, like old balloons days after a party.

Muntaha picked up a sack and marched to her Nana Jani.

"Look at this!" Muntaha held up a sack with barely any grain in it at all. "We used to have such a huge harvest. Now, there is so little. Don't say it's not true, because I have proof!"

Nana Jani sighed and took hold of Muntaha's hand. "My dear girl. You see how I am getting older? The land is getting older too. It gets less productive as the years go by. The nutritious topsoil, which is wonderful for growing plants, slowly erodes away."

Nana Jani held Muntaha's hand and together they walked to the field. The field has been plowed after the harvest and all that remained was bare, loose soil. Grandfather picked up some stones from the field.

"Years ago," Grandfather began, "These stones were once buried deep beneath a layer of soft soil. Now, after each harvest, the soil slowly gets washed away by the rain. These rocks are all that is left behind."

Why was wind and rain causing problems for Nana Jani and his field?

Think, Pair, Share!

Part 4

Muntaha's brilliant idea

Muntaha wanted to help. She thought as hard as she could. There was something that Nana Jani had said earlier which gave Muntaha a brilliant idea!

"I know!" Muntaha exclaimed. "What if we left wheat stalks or straw in the field between planting seasons? The dry plant stalks will break the wind. The roots will keep the rain from washing away the top soil. After a harvest, the plant stalks will protect the field, just like your tickly beard protects your face!"

Why did Muntaha suggest leaving the roots and stalks in the field after harvest?

Think, Pair, Share!

"What an amazing idea!" Nana Jani exclaimed. "I will stop trimming the field after harvest time. The field will have a tickly Nana Jani beard just like me!" he said with a smile.

From that day onwards, after the harvest they made sure to leave the the plant stalks and roots behind to protect the ground from winter's harsh winds and strong rains.

They removed rocks from the field and fertilized the soil. Their soil was rich and fertile once again. At harvest time, the sacks of grain were filled and stretched tight. When Nana Jani hugged Muntaha, she was the one tickling him with a beautiful golden wheat stalk!

What did they do to make the field fertile again?

Think, Pair, Share!

Old sediments form new rocks

Over time, old sediment layers become buried deep under new sediment layers. After millions of years, the soft sediments slowly harden to become new sedimentary rocks.

The layers of sedimentary rock in this cliff side were once loose river sediments.

Can you identify different sedimentary layers in this cliff side? How many layers do you see?

Do sedimentary rocks form quickly or slowly?

Earth events can shape new land

Cut and fold the flaps to see how Earth events can shape new land.

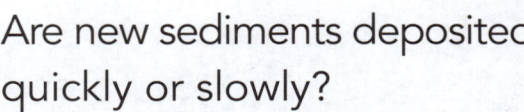

Are new sediments deposited quickly or slowly?

Is this change fast or slow?

Fold Line

Do volcanic eruptions happen fast or slow?

Is this change fast or slow?

Fold Line

Do earthquakes happen fast or slow?

Is this change fast or slow?

Fold Line

39

Rivers quickly carry sediments downhill that come to rest in low areas, creating new layers of ground.

Volcanic eruptions happen fast, in a matter of minutes. Over thousands of years, volcanic islands can form. This island was slowly made by a volcano.

Earthquakes happen fast, in a matter of minutes. Slowly, over millions of years, earthquakes can push up entire mountain ranges.

Uluru Rock is made up of sediments

Uluru Rock is made of ancient sediments that were buried deep underground forming sedimentary rocks. Those rocks were pushed up to the surface by earthquake activity. Now the rocks are being eroded away by rainwater.

Do you think the natural process that formed Uluru Rock happened fast or slow? Why do you think so?

_____

_____

_____

_____

_____

Explore the
Phenomenon!

A volcanic eruption happens quickly

Ash flies up high in the sky as this volcano erupts. Lava also flows out from the crater. Volcanic eruptions such as these can happen quickly—in a few seconds, minutes or days. This is a very short time compared to other geologic events.

Explore:

"Volcán de Fuego, Guatemala"

Explore Google Earth to find the following features on Volcán de Fuego.

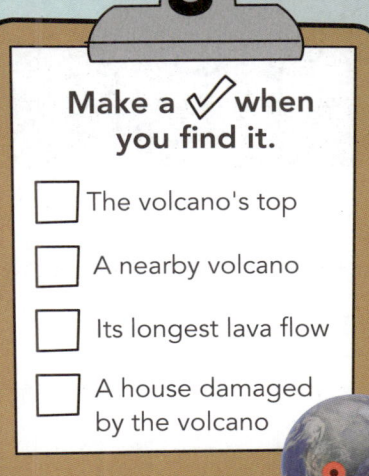

Make a ✓ when you find it.

☐ The volcano's top

☐ A nearby volcano

☐ Its longest lava flow

☐ A house damaged by the volcano

Do you think each of the events in the checklist happened fast or slow?

Think, Pair, Share!

Volcán de Fuego, in Guatemala, is known for its consistent eruptions. Small eruptions of gas and ash occur every 15 to 20 minutes. Larger eruptions are more rare and only happen about once every ten years.

Credit: Juan Francisco

Lava comes out of Volcán de Fuego in Guatemala.

Does a volcanic eruption commonly happen fast or slow?

Smoke and ash come out from the top of Volcán de Fuego in Guatemala.

An island's formation happens slowly

The Hawaiian Islands were formed by volcanic eruptions. During an eruption, hot lava flows out of the ground and cools to make new land. The Kilauea volcano has been actively erupting for a very long time. It has taken over half a million years for volcanic eruptions to create the big island of Hawaii.

Explore:

Google Earth

"The Island of Hawaii"

Explore Google Earth to find the following features in Hawaii.

Make a ✓ when you find it.

☐ Eight Hawaiian Islands

☐ A volcanic crater

☐ Black rock (lava flow)

☐ Two big volcanos

Did each of the events in the checklist happen quickly or slowly?

Think, Pair, Share!